VOLUME 1

Music Reading
A Comprehensive Approach

VERNON L. KLIEWER

School of Music
Indiana University

PRENTICE-HALL, INC., Englewood Cliffs, New Jersey

To my wife Diane

and

Konrad, Julie, and Rebecca

Printed in the United States of America

ISBN: 0-13-607903-2

Library of Congress Catalog Card. No.: 72-3870

10   9   8   7   6   5   4   3   2   1

179555

PRENTICE-HALL INTERNATIONAL, INC., London
PRENTICE-HALL OF AUSTRALIA, PTY. LTD., Sydney
PRENTICE-HALL OF CANADA, LTD., Toronto
PRENTICE-HALL OF INDIA PRIVATE LIMITED, New Delhi
PRENTICE-HALL OF JAPAN, INC., Tokyo

Contents

Preface

vii

Unit 1

1

RHYTHM: *Division of the Beat in Simple Meters*
PITCH: *Four-Note Sets*
LEAPS: *Step Motion Predominates*
TEXTURE: *One and Two Parts*
RANGE: *Generally a Fourth*

Unit 2

18

RHYTHM: *Division and Subdivision of the Beat*
in Simple and Compound Meters
PITCH: *Four- and Five-Note Sets*
LEAPS: *Third, Fourth and Fifth*
Step Motion Predominates
TEXTURE: *One and Two Parts*
RANGE: *Generally a Fifth*

Unit 3

35

RHYTHM: *Introduction of Asymmetric Groupings*
PITCH: *Introduction of Six-Note Set*
LEAPS: *Third (Single and Consecutive), Fourth and Fifth*
Step Motion Predominates
TEXTURE: *One to Three Parts*
RANGE: *Occasionally a Seventh*

Unit 4

54

RHYTHM: *Introduction of Interbeat Syncopation*
PITCH: *As in Unit 3*

iii

LEAPS: *As in Unit 3*
TEXTURE: *One to Three Parts*
RANGE: *Up to an Octave*

Unit 5
74

RHYTHM: *Continues Interbeat Syncopation*
Introduction of Intrabeat Syncopation
PITCH: *Five- and Six-Note Sets*
Sets Containing Two Adjacent Half Steps
LEAPS: *As in Preceding Units*
TEXTURE: *One to Three Parts*
RANGE: *Generally an Octave*

Unit 6
98

RHYTHM: *As in Preceding Units*
PITCH: *Five- to Seven-Note Sets*
Sets Containing Two Adjacent Half Steps
LEAPS: *Third, Fourth, Fifth, Sixth, and Octave*
Step Motion Predominates
TEXTURE: *One to Three Parts*
RANGE: *Generally an Octave*

Unit 7
123

RHYTHM: *As in Preceding Units*
Irregular Groupings in Conventional Meters
PITCH: *Sets Used in Preceding Units*
LEAPS: *As in Preceding Units*
TEXTURE: *One to Three Parts*
RANGE: *Generally an Octave*

Unit 8
147

RHYTHM: *As in Preceding Units*
PITCH: *Sets Used in Preceding Units*
Sets Containing Three Adjacent Half Steps
LEAPS: *As in Preceding Units*
TEXTURE: *One to Four Parts*
RANGE: *Generally an Octave*

Unit 9
174

RHYTHM: *Introduction of Intrabeat Triplet and Duplet*
PITCH: *As in Preceding Units*
LEAPS: *As in Preceding Units with Occasional Tritones*
TEXTURE: *As in Preceding Units*
RANGE: *Generally a Ninth*

Unit 10
203

RHYTHM: *Introduction of Interbeat Triplets and Duplets*
PITCH: *Sets Used in Preceding Units*
LEAPS: *Introduction of Leaps of a Seventh*
TEXTURE: *One to Four Parts*
RANGE: *Generally a Tenth*

Unit 11
232

RHYTHM: *Introduction of Intrabeat Quadruplets*
PITCH: *Sets Used in Preceding Units*
and Sets Containing Four Consecutive Half Steps
LEAPS: *As in Preceding Units*
TEXTURE: *As in Preceding Units*
RANGE: *Generally an Eleventh*

Unit 12
260

RHYTHM: *Introduction of Intrabeat Three-Against-Two*
and Four-Against-Three
PITCH: *Sets Used in Preceding Units*
LEAPS: *As in Preceding Units*
TEXTURE: *As in Preceding Units*
RANGE: *Generally a Twelfth*

Unit 13
286

RHYTHM: *Continuation of Preceding Units*
PITCH: *Sets Used in Preceding Units*
LEAPS: *As in Preceding Units with Emphasis on Tritone*
TEXTURE: *One to Four Parts*
RANGE: *As in Preceding Unit*

Unit 14
314

RHYTHM: *Introduction of Interbeat Four-Against-Three*
PITCH: *Sets As in Preceding Units*
Sets Containing Five Consecutive Half Steps
LEAPS: *As in Preceding Units*
TEXTURE: *As in Preceding Units*
RANGE: *Generally a Twelfth*

Preface

Fluency in music reading is essential for a musician: it develops aural imagery; it stimulates and reinforces aural perception; it enhances musical understanding; it reduces the time needed to learn new works; it contributes to musical self-dependency; it leads to skill in sight reading.

With these goals as an objective, this volume contains a wide range of materials and activities, both "composed" for the occasion and taken from music literature, to aid the student in becoming a proficient music reader. Each of the units is organized to provide exposure to a variety of musical styles within systematically imposed limitations. These limitations are based on the number of elements making up a particular musical dimension, e.g., pitch.

In Unit 2 the pitch materials are four- and five-note sets[1] containing a single half step; in Unit 11 the pitch materials include sets having four consecutive half steps; In Unit 2 there are no leaps larger than a fifth; in Unit 11, leaps of a seventh are a part of the musical contexts. Initially, the range of individual lines is restricted to a small span; eventually, the range is increased so that no limitations are imposed. Beginning with the first unit the sound materials are used in both serial and non-serial contexts. Most of the musical examples in early units, whether serial or not, have pitch focus, a result of the presentation order of pitch materials. Pitch focus as a factor in musical organization is represented by many types of musical examples, each of which is intended to reveal patterning which produces this phenomenon, whether it occurs in a Gregorian melody or in a work by Stravinsky.

Musical contexts in which pitch focus is absent or ambiguous appear from the first unit, particularly in the examples composed for the two volumes. These composed examples provide preparation well in advance for the more complex non-tonal examples taken from music literature that appear in later units. In either case, the pitch materials are organized into "functional" and "non-functional" musical configurations.

The side-by-side presentation of different approaches to musical organization resembles daily musical experiences. Similarly, the methods brought to bear in developing reading fluency relate to many sources.[2] Basic to any music-reading procedure is immediate recognition of contextual patterns, in essence an analytic approach. The patterns recognized may be minute, such as ♩. ♪ | ♩ , or a four-note pitch pattern framed by a perfect fourth, or of the magnitude of an entire phrase or section. The aural imagery necessary for one context may be only partially applicable to another. For example, in many melodic patterns an ascending perfect fourth is correctly imaged with the upper note as tonic; to bring this same imagery to *all* occurrences of perfect fourth intervals introduces extraneous fac-

---

[1] Set = a collection of notes.

[2] The author does not rule out any useful procedure. For example, the analytic and aural awareness of a *tonality frame* (Ch. 2, *Materials and Structure of Music*, Vol. 1, Christ, *et al.*, Prentice-Hall, Inc.) is extremely useful for tonal music, as is the awareness of harmonic structure for music in major and minor keys. On the other hand, to *impose* a supposed harmonic structure on a context in which it is *not* a structural factor adds complexities which are intellectual, not musical.

tors that may hinder the formation of appropriate aural images. What is appropriate for a given context and individual is highly variable; this book provides for the discovery of appropriate means.[3]

It is assumed that the student has had considerable experience with music, both as a performer and as a listener, and that he has knowledge of music fundamentals, both in theory and in practice. These volumes are not designed to teach music fundamentals of the type normally considered essential prior to enrolling in a college or university music curriculum; rather, they provide a systematic plan for improving musicianship through becoming a better reader. Consistent with this, the book contains little in the way of expository explanations.

Rhythm and pitch are emphasized, but materials are provided for reading in which loudness (dynamics), color (timbre), or density (texture) are important factors. Some of the examples from literature, in terms of range, are not entirely singable, but much reading practice can be derived from *approximating* the contours vocally, by whistling, or by making music with other sound sources[4] while performing other dimensions of the example precisely. Some of the exercises in this collection specify sound sources other than vocal. In some instances the sounds are prescribed, but these prescriptions may be changed at the discretion of the instructor. It is suggested that instruments be used to perform some of the examples or some of the parts in multi-part examples to make the reading experience more like the musical experience.

Each of the units deals with particular types of problems and each unit draws on materials and procedures from preceding units. In brief, rhythmic matters are presented first, followed by pitch matters and then the combination of rhythm and pitch into musical configurations. The isolation into dimensions, their order of appearance, and the types of examples do not dictate the order of class presentation, but provide one particular arrangement. The composed examples present possible contexts; the examples from literature present actual contexts. The actual musical contexts of a unit may have been prepared for in previous units; similarly, the composed examples may prepare for later eventualities.

These volumes are designed with flexibility in mind. In some situations it is conceivable that a unit would occupy approximately two weeks; on the other hand, some situations would require more time, or even less. It is the teacher who must decide when a unit has been mastered. In any event, a student who masters the contents will be a proficient reader.

[3] For more detailed discussion on the use of the book see the Teacher's Manual.

[4] Music reading and sight reading are more than sight singing. Music reading is the acquisition of skill in the reading of music, which may be acquired through singing, clapping, tapping, dancing, or realizing musical shapes in some way other than that designated by notation. Sight reading is a test in reading skill (by no means the only one, or the best). Sight singing is the use of the vocal mechanism in the testing process.

Unit 1

RHYTHM: *Division of the Beat in Simple Meters*
PITCH: *Four-Note Sets*
LEAPS: *Step Motion Predominates*
TEXTURE: *One and Two Parts*
RANGE: *Generally a Fourth*

RHYTHM

Practice Rhythm Patterns

Rhythm Phrases

Performance procedure suggestions:

1. Recite with a vocable such as "ta."
2. Use a pitch (monotone style) for each articulation, alternating pitches or another variant, e.g.:

3. Adopt various dynamic schemes, e.g.:

$$p \quad \diagup\!\!\!\!f \; ; \quad mf \quad \diagup\!\!\!\!ff \quad \diagdown \; ; \quad \text{etc.}$$

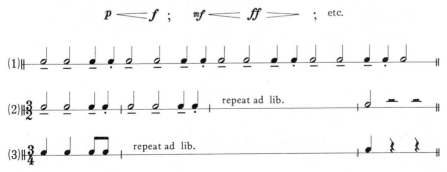

1

2

Practice Rhythm Patterns

Performance procedure suggestions:

1. Recite with a vocable such as "ta" or "la."

2. Use pitch patterns such as

*Rhythm Phrases**

* To aid in the development of fluency, impose various types of dynamic schemes on the phrase-rhythms. The reading process will be helped most if the scheme chosen is notated in pencil by the student in the manner shown.

5

PITCH

Four-Note Pitch Sets

Performance procedure suggestions:

1. Students should learn the sets by hearing them performed by the instructor. The patterns may be presented vocally or instrumentally in a step arrangement as notated or with the notes in various orders, e.g.:

2. Any order used for first set may apply also to sets 2 and 3.

Pitch Patterns

Pitch Phrases

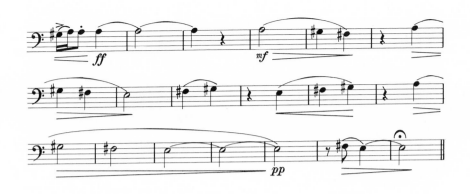

13

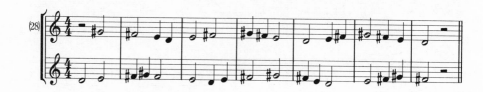

Unit 2

RHYTHM: *Division and Subdivision of the Beat
in Simple and Compound Meters*
PITCH: *Four- and Five-Note Sets*
LEAPS: *Third, Fourth and Fifth*
Step Motion Predominates
TEXTURE: *One and Two Parts*
RANGE: *Generally a Fifth*

RHYTHM

Practice Rhythm Patterns

Rhythm Phrases

* Notation designates approximate melodic contours; the rise and fall of the line represents highs and lows in relation to the "middle" note, which is the note falling on the line.

* = Clap
**= Approximate melodic contour

PITCH

Four- and Five-Note Pitch Sets*

Pitch Patterns

* See page 1 for practice suggestions.

Pitch Phrases

From "Larghetto." (c) 1956, Consolidated Music Publishers, Inc.—Volume 17, *Music for Millions* Series "Easy Classics to Moderns." Compiled and Edited by Denes Agay. Used by Permission.

29

* ⸸ = Clap

31

33

From *Guia Pratico,* "O Anel."

Unit 3

RHYTHM: *Introduction of Asymmetric Groupings*
PITCH: *Introduction of Six-Note Set*
LEAPS: *Third (Single and Consecutive), Fourth and Fifth*
Step Motion Predominates
TEXTURE: *One to Three Parts*
RANGE: *Occasionally a Seventh*

RHYTHM

Practice Rhythm Patterns

Rhythm Phrases

35

37

Six-Note Pitch Sets

Pitch Patterns

41

E, dame jolie

Reprinted by permission of the publishers from Archibald T. Davison & Willi Apel, eds. *Historical Anthology of Music,* Volume I. *Cambridge, Mass.: Harvard University Press,* Copyright 1946, 1949, by the President and Fellows of Harvard College.

O Roma noblis (Goliard)

Guillaume d'Amiens

Reprinted by permission of the publishers from Archibald T. Davison & Willi Apel, eds. *Historical Anthology of Music,* Volume I. *Cambridge, Mass.: Harvard University Press,* Copyright, 1946, 1949, by the President and Fellows of Harvard College.

(22) *Bartók*

From *Seven Sketches*, No. 2, Op. 9
Copyright 1950 by Boosey & Hawkes Inc.
Reprinted by permission.

(23) *Orff*

𝅘𝅥 =120

f sempre ben declamato

From "Fortune Plango Vulnera" in *Carmine Burana*
Copyright © 1937 by B. Schott's Soehne
Copyright renewed 1965 by B. Schott's Soehne
Used by Permission

(24) Slow *Traditional*

(25) *Traditional*

45

German

Ach El - se-lein, lie - bes El - se-lein mein, wie gern wär ich___ bei dir, wie gern___ wär ich bei dir; so sind___ zwei tie - fe Was - ser wohl zwi - schen dir und mir, so sind___ zwei tie - fe Was - ser wohl zwi - schen dir und mir.

♪=168

Seminole

46

Mussorgsky

Acalanto ♪=152   arr. de H. Villa-Lobos

(42)

Mu - ca -ma bo - ni -ta, Vin-da da Ba - í - a, To - ma êste me

Mu - ca -ma bo - ni -ta, Vin-da da Ba - í - a, To - ma êste me

ni - no, La - vai na ba - ci - a! Mu - ci - a!   Ah!

ni - no, La - vai na ba - ci - a! Mu - ci - a!   Ah!

From *Guia Pratico,* "Higiene."

Ductia

(43)

Voice   Schütz

(44)

Evang: Spricht Pi - lat - tus zu ih - nen; *Pilatus:* Soll ich eu -ren Kö - nig

Instrument

keru - zi - gen *Evang:* Die Ho-hen-prie - ster ant - wor - te - ten:

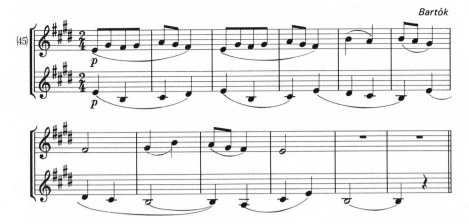

Bartók

From *Forty-Four Violin Duos* # 1
Copyright 1933 by Universal Edition, Vienna. Renewed 1960.
Copyright and Renewal assigned to Boosey & Hawkes Inc., for the U.S.A.
Reprinted by permission.

179555

From "In Three Parts"
Copyright 1941 by Hawkes & Son (London) Ltd. Renewed 1967.
Reprinted by permission of Boosey & Hawkes Inc.

Unit 4

RHYTHM: *Introduction of Interbeat Syncopation*
PITCH: *As in Unit 3*
LEAPS: *As in Unit 3*
TEXTURE: *One to Three Parts*
RANGE: *Up to an Octave*

RHYTHM

Practice Rhythm Patterns

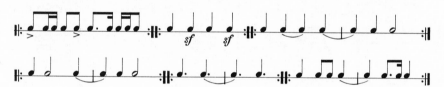

Rhythm Phrases

54

Very sustained

58

PITCH

Six-Note Pitch Sets

(17) Papago

(18) Spain

Duer - me ni - ño chi - qui - to_____

duer - me mi al - ma_____ duer - me - te

lu - ce - ri - to de la ma - ña - na._____

(19) Midwestern

(20) Allegro ♩=144 Mussorgsky

Gafurius

Mussorgsky

69

Juan Orrego-Salas

Reprinted by permission of the composer.

IMPROVISATION

a. Invent several different melodies based on the information given for each of the problems.*

Trombone, bassoon (or other instru.) or voice

*These improvisation exercises are drills in tonal memory and melodic shape. Before attempting any of the problems, the student should know the pitch materials. No leaps larger than a fifth should be used; tertian triad outlining may be employed if it seems appropriate. If the student desires, a one-line serial accompaniment may be improvised for *3a* and *3b*.

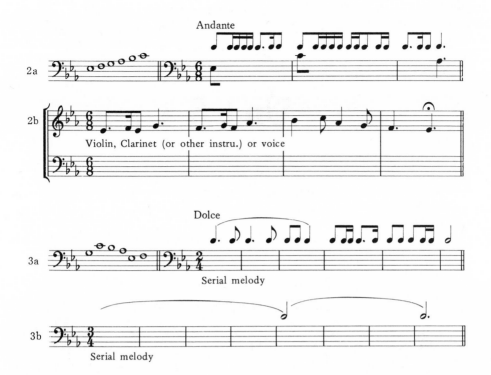

Unit 5

RHYTHM: *Continues Interbeat Syncopation*
Introduction of Intrabeat Syncopation
PITCH: *Five- and Six-note Sets*
Sets Containing Two Adjacent Half Steps
LEAPS: *As in Preceding Units*
TEXTURE: *One to Three Parts*
RANGE: *Generally an Octave*

RHYTHM

Practice Rhythm Patterns

Rhythm Phrases

81

PITCH

Six-Note Pitch Sets.

Pitch Patterns

* Beginning with this unit, only the pitch sets appearing for the first time will be shown in scalar form. For review purposes, refer to the pitch sets and preparatory patterns of the preceding units.

Pitch Phrases

From "Pastorale" in *Enfantines*. Reprinted by permission of the copyright owner.
Copyright MCMXXIV by Carl Fischer, Inc., New York.

From *For Children*
Copyright 1946 by Boosey & Hawkes Inc.
Reprinted by permission.

"Gewan ich ze minnen ie quoten wân" from Seagrave and Thomas, *The Songs of the Minnesingers*. Reprinted by permission of the University of Illinois Press.

ouch wi - der__ ko - men mit nih - te__ kan und

al - sô mit sor - gen die__ zît__ hin - ver - trî - bet

(17) *Ute*

(18) *Spain*

Es - te ni - ño tie - ne sue - ño tie - ne ga - nas de dor -

mir, tie ne un o - ji - to ce - rra - do, yo - tro no lo pue - de a -

brir, nie - ve en el ca - mi - no, nie - ve en la he - re - dad

duér - me - te mi ni - ño, que ne - van - do es tá.__

Letelier

(19) Tranquillo

Des - can - sa Vir - gen di - cho - sa flor del ver - gel__ ce - les - tial__ que es

to - do un Dios quien re - pò - sa en tu se - no vir - gi - nal__ Des -

From "Descansa Virgen Dichosa." Reprinted by permission of the composer.

Martinu

(20)

P dolce

From *Sonata No. 2 for Violoncello and Piano*. Reprinted by permission of Associated Music Publishers, Inc.

Josquin des Prés

Dvořák

Andante moderato ♩ = ca.80

(28)

Fine

D.C. al Fine

From "Shall I Die for Mannis Sake." Copyright 1967 by Boosey & Hawkes Music Publishers Ltd.

Reprinted by permission of Boosey & Hawkes Inc.

Monteverdi

(29)

* The leap may be changed to unison by singing an octave lower.

From "79 Chorales" (Opus 28) by Marcel Dupré
Copyrighted 1932, by The H. W. Gray Co., Inc.
Renewed 1960. Used by Permission.

* If necessary, the octave leap may be practiced in advance. Unit 6 contains other examples with octave leaps.

** The pedal part may be played (e.g., on a cello, trombone, etc.) or sung. If sung, those phrases which are too low may be sung an octave higher.

IMPROVISATION

Invent melodies based on the information given for each of the problems.

These are drills in tonal memory and melodic shape. Before attempting them, know the pitch materials. No leaps larger than a fifth should be used; tertian triad outlining may occur if it seems appropriate. If the student desires, one-line serial accompaniments may be improvised for *3a* and *3b*.

Unit 6

RHYTHM: *As in Preceding Units*
PITCH: *Five- to Seven-Note Sets*
Sets Containing Two Adjacent Half Steps
LEAPS: *Third, Fourth, Fifth, Sixth, and Octave*
Step Motion Predominates
TEXTURE: *One to Three Parts*
RANGE: *Generally an Octave*

RHYTHM

Practice Rhythm Patterns

Rhythm Phrases

*♩ = "Tap or "la"

✗ = Clap

Adagio; legato throughout

(17)

Presto

(18)

*♩= Tap on wood
♩= Tap on book
♪= Tap on metal

PITCH

Seven-Note Pitch Sets

Pitch Patterns

Pitch Phrases

American

Troubadour

Mussorgsky

Tempo giusto ♩ = 84

Hungary

Langsam — Brahms (15)

Moderato — Chile (16)

Canon — Alpine (17)

Alegre — Chile (18)

Allegro con moto   *Chabrier*

Bartók

From "Song No. 4" from *Four Slovak Folk Songs*

Piano throughout (breathe when required)

Moderato con moto — Chausson

Un peu plus lent

"Le Charme." Courtesy of International Music Company, New York, New York.

Brahms (Folk)

Slowly (canon for two voices)

Persichetti

The pri-ma-ry el - e - ment of a can-on—— is not the score but the mel - o-dy. The ca-non - ic set -ting should

From "Preface to Canons."
© Copyright 1947 Music Press, Inc.
Reprinted by permission of the Theodore Presser Company.

113

not be tried be-forethe mel-o-dy___ is com-plete-ly mas-

tered. It is de-plor-a-ble if a pian-o is

nec-es-sa-ry for___ stud-y-ing the tune; it is en-tire-ly out

of the ques-tion to use the pian-o for the pol-y-phon-ic

set-up. This has to be done a-

-cap-pel-la___

Andantino

Haydn (adapted)

(30)

Argentina

La es-tre - lla que me a-lum - bra - ba   Par - tes al a - ma - ne -

Solo   Estribillo

cer   ya   no la   pue - do en-con - trar_____   tris - te me -

que - do y no   sé   que he de ha   cer

*  = Tap on wood   = Tap on metal

    = Tap on book   = Clap

IMPROVISATION

Invent melodies based on the information given for each of the problems.

On first and third beats added part should form a 3rd or 5th with given parts.

Sing given melody; second person sings
improvised accompaniment.

Unit 7

RHYTHM: *As in Preceding Units*
Irregular Groupings in Conventional Meters
PITCH: *Sets Used in Preceding Units*
LEAPS: *As in Preceding Units*
TEXTURE: *One to Three Parts*
RANGE: *Generally an Octave*

RHYTHM

Practice Rhythm Patterns

Rhythm Phrases

125

* ♩ = Clap

* ♩ = Tap on wood

  ♩ = Tap on book

PITCH

Seven-Note Pitch Sets

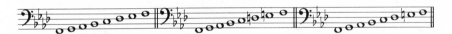

Pitch Patterns*

Pitch Phrases

* Add the necessary accidentals to use the pitches of each of the pitch-sets.

131

From "Thy Word With Me Shall Always Stay" in *Devotional Song Series*, *No. 951*. Reprinted by permission of Augsburg Publishing House, Minneapolis, Minnesota, copyright owners.

"Lanc bin ich gewews et verdâht" from Seagrave and Thomas, *The Songs of the Minnesingers*. Reprinted by permission of the University of Illinois Press.

win - nen von der fro - wen mîn. Wie möhte
ich danne trû - ric sîn? Ob ir rô - ter
munt tuot mir fröi - de kunt, sô ge-
trûre ich nie - mer mê: êst quit, was mir wê.

Spain

(17)

Rossi

(18)

pp

Sehr rasch   *Schumann*

(19)   *f*

Es treibt mich

Langsamer

hin, es treibt mich her! Noch we - ni - ge Stun - den, dann

soll ich sie schau-en, sie sel-ber, die schön-ste der schö-nen Jung-frau-en:

Du ar-mes Herz, was pochst du schwer? Die Stun-den sind a-ber ein fau-les Volk! Schle-ppen sich be-hag-lich trä-ge, schlei-chen gäh-nend ih-re We-ge: tumm-le dich, du fau-les Volk!

To-ben-de Ei-le mich trei-bend er-fasst! A-ber wohl nie-mals lieb-ten die Ho-ren, nie-mals, nie-mals lieb-ten die Ho-ren; heim-lich im grau-sa-men Ban-de ver-schwo-ren, spot-ten sie tück-isch der Lie-ben-den Hast.

From "Western Winds"
© Copyright 1947 Music Press, Inc.
Reprinted by permission of the Theodore Presser Company.

136

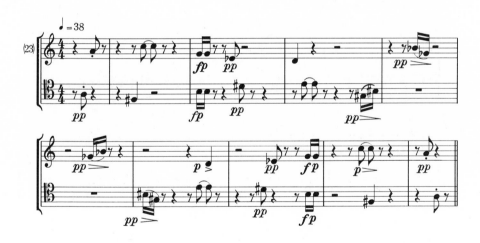

137

J. K. F. Fischer

138

From *Of Beasts*. Reprinted by permission of G. Schirmer, Inc.

| Los | frau, | und | hör | des | hor | - | nes | schal, perg | und |
| Mich | rüert | ain | wind | von | o | - | ri | - ent, der | ent - |

"Sag an, herzlieb, nu was bededeutet" from Seagrave and Thomas, *The Songs of the Minnesingers*. Reprinted by permission of the University of Illinois Press.

"Sag an herz - lieb, nu was be - deu - tet uns so
"Ai - ni - ger man, sol uns der gast er - stö - ren

tal ü - ber - al a - ne qual, auch
rent auch plent das fir - ma - ment, und

gar schrick li - cher hal
hie so ach el - lend?

hör ich die nach - ti - gal, des liech - ten
der uns die freud hie went. zart min - nik -

mit sei - nem don?"
wem last du mich?"

mor - gen rö - te sich vor der pläw her dringt. plas
li - che die - ren, das ho - ren poll - ret grim - mik -

a - a - hü, a - a - hü
a - a hü, a - a - hü

schon wach - ter! ich spür dein zo -
lich. ich hör dich wol, du truebst

wol - auff die na - cken ploss.
her - get des ta - ges schein. Pald ab dem weg,

ren mi - chel gross.
die frau - e mein. Los

140

die ge - ren läg. hör hör, hör, ge - sell, klueg - li - chen, ge -
los, los, los, sen - lei - che klag, mord - li - cher
schell,
tag, wie lang sol un - ser not mit
stand up, risch up, snell up. die
dir be - stan?
vog - lin klin - gen in dem hard, am - sel dro - schel, der
hab ur - laub, hö - chster
vink und ain zei - se - lein, das nen - net sich gug - guk.
schatz, kurz - lich her - wi - der - ruck.

(29) Trio a 2 Oboi e Fagotto   *J. S. Bach*

Oboe I

Oboe II

Fagotto

Andante   *Pasquini*

(30)

Canon a trè

Rohwer

(31)

Adagio

(32)

* + =Tap on wood ✶ = Clap   1st repeat, 1 takes   2nd repeat, 2 takes

   ⊦ = Tap on book   3, 2 takes 1, and   3, 3 takes 1, and

                                   3 takes 2;   1 takes 2.

IMPROVISATION

Invent melodies based on the information given for each of the problems.

The improvised part should form a third or fifth with the given parts.

Play the given melody on a clarinet or oboe; the second person sings an improvised accompaniment.

Accompaniment pitch materials derived from (1) Phrygian, (2) minor, and (3) major. The three accompaniments should be made by three different persons. Rhythm ratio should be predominantly 2:1.

6-note row.   Invent a serial melody based on the *P** and *R** forms of the 6-note row.

    * *P* = Prime (original) form of the row.
        R = Retrograde of the prime form of the row.

146

Unit 8

RHYTHM: *As in Preceding Units*
PITCH: *Sets Used in Preceding Units*
Sets Containing Three Adjacent Half Steps
LEAPS: *As in Preceding Units*
TEXTURE: *One to Four Parts*
RANGE: *Generally an Octave*

RHYTHM

Practice Rhythm Patterns

Rhythm Phrases

*⊥ = Tap on wood; taps may be alternated between the hands

✶ = Clap

148

* + = Tap on wood

✗ = Clap

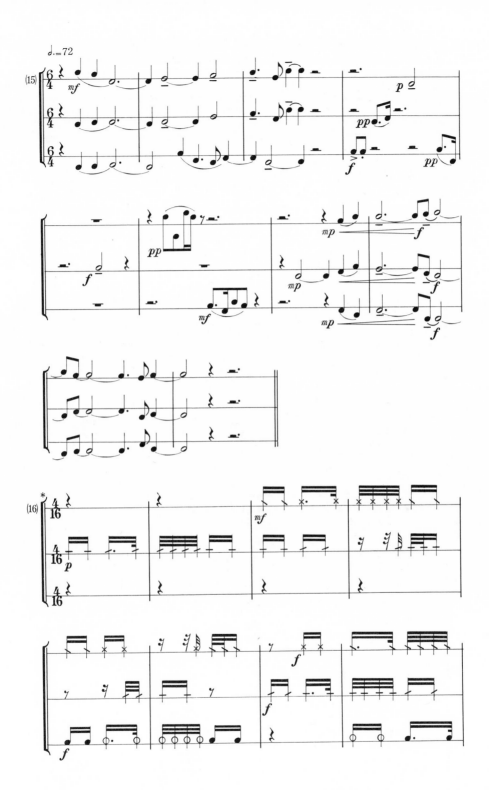

151

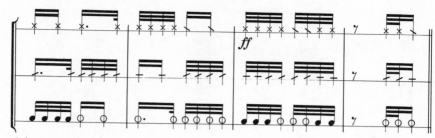

* ┼ = Tap on wood
 ┼ = Tap on book
 ┼ = Tap on metal
 ✻ = Hand Clap
 φ = Slap

PITCH

Pitch Sets*

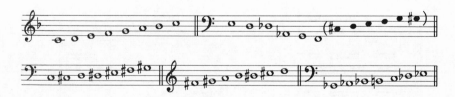

* Use pitch patterns in units 6 and 7 for drill with mixolydian materials.

Pitch Patterns

Pitch Phrases

156

157

"Day of Judgment" from *Down-East Spirituals and Others,* ed. Geo. Pullen Jackson. Reprinted by permission of the publisher, J. J. Augustin.

"Wedding Song" from *Poniky*.
Copyright 1924 by Universal Edition, Vienna. Renewed 1951.
Copyright assigned to Boosey & Hawkes Ltd. for all countries.
Reprinted by permission of Boosey & Hawkes Inc.

159

From *Guia Pratico*, "Vamos, Maninha."

mar... Va-mos ver a lan-cha no-va Que do céu ca-iu no mar.

J. S. Bach

Voice

(21)

Continuo

♩=68

(22)

From "We Gather Up In This Brief Hour." Reprinted by permission of Bärenreiter Verlag.

Andante con moto

(26)

Mussorgsky

164

Preis sei dem ew' - gen Herrn!
Fa - ther of Heav'n and earth!

und
ry!

165

Schubert

Guillaume de Machaut

IMPROVISATION

Invent melodies based on the information given for each problem.

171

1) On the beat articulations of melody form third or sixth with lowest sounding part.

2) On the beat articulations of melody form fourth or fifth with lowest sounding part.

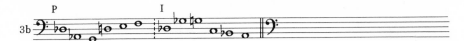

Use both *P** and *I** forms of the row; begin with either *P* or *I*. Use any of the rhythm phrases appearing in this unit. If desired, the two forms of the row may be used in two- or three-part rhythm phrases.

* *P* = Prime (original) form of the row.
  I = Inverted form of the prime.

Unit 9

RHYTHM: *Introduction of Intrabeat Triplet and Duplet*
PITCH: *As in Preceding Units*
LEAPS: *As in Preceding Units with Occasional Tritones*
TEXTURE: *As in Preceding Units*
RANGE: *Generally a Ninth*

RHYTHM

Practice Rhythm Patterns*

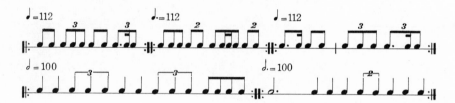

Rhythm Phrases

* To achieve accuracy in the performance of triplets and duplets, subdivide the beat to provide a common denominator; e.g.:

174

175

* ✻ = Clap

φ = Slap

*
♩ = Tap on metal
♩ = Tap on book

179

✳ = Clap

φ = Slap

PITCH

Pitch Sets

Pitch Patterns

Pitch Phrases

183

185

Etwas langsam

Brahms

Sweden

Allegro vivace (♩ = 144)

arr. by Villa-Lobos
Moderato

rall.

From *Guia Pratico,* "Pombinha, Rolinha."

Chile

From "With Rue My Heart Is Laden." Reprinted by permission of G. Schirmer, Inc.

"Mandoline." Copyright MCMXIII by Oliver Ditson Company.
Reprinted by permission.

Aimeric de Peguillam

Andante non troppo ♩.= 84

Mussorgsky

(23)

dolce

f

J. S. Bach

(24)

189

L. Mozart

* Notes in parentheses: percussive sounds as indicated, or similar to those indicated.

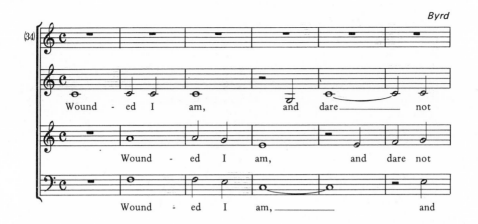

(34) Wound - ed I am, and dare_____ not

Wound - ed I am, and dare not

Wound - ed I am,_____ and

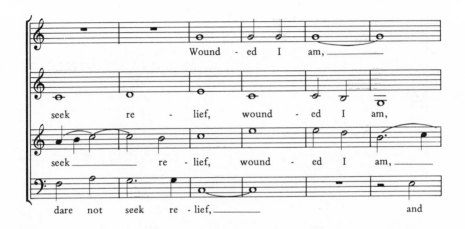

Wound - ed I am,_____

seek re - lief, wound - ed I am,

seek_____ re - lief, wound - ed I am,_____

dare not seek re - lief,_____ and

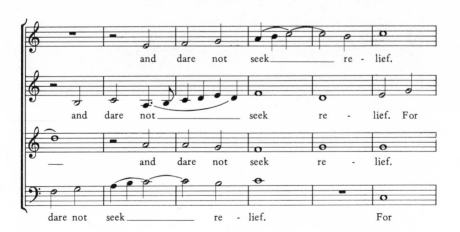

and dare not seek_____ re - lief.

and dare not_____ seek re - lief. For

____ and dare not seek re - lief.

dare not seek_____ re - lief. For

From "Two Songs of Spring." Music by Bernhard Heiden, text by Samuel Yellen.

© Copyright 1966 by Continuo Music Press, Inc.
Used by permission of
Continuo Music Press, Inc.
Sole Agent—Alexander Broude, Inc.

IMPROVISATION

Invent melodies based on the information given for each problem.

1) On the beat articulations of melody form third or sixth with lowest part.

2) On the beat articulations of melody form fourth or fifth with lowest part.

Use both *P** *and I** forms of the row: begin with either *P* or *I*. Use any of the rhythm phrases appearing in this unit. If desired, the two forms of the row may be used with any of the two-, three-, or four-part rhythm phrases.

* *P* = Prime (original) form of the row.
  I = Inverted form of the prime.

Unit 10

RHYTHM: *Introduction of Interbeat Triplets and Duplets*
PITCH: *Sets Used in Preceding Units*
LEAPS: *Introduction of Leaps of a Seventh*
TEXTURE: *One to Four Parts*
RANGE: *Generally a Tenth*

RHYTHM

Practice Rhythm Patterns

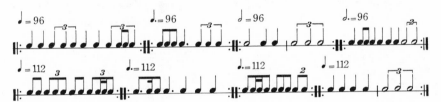

Rhythm Phrases

205

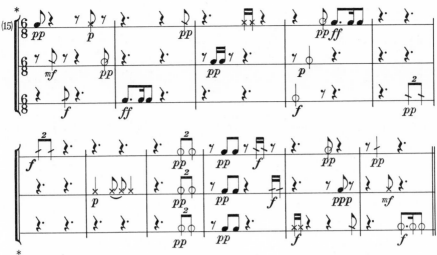

* ⁊ = Tap on book
⁊ = Tap on metal
⁑ = Clap
ϕ = Slap

207

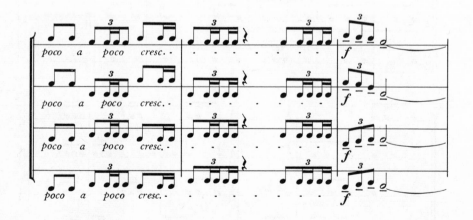

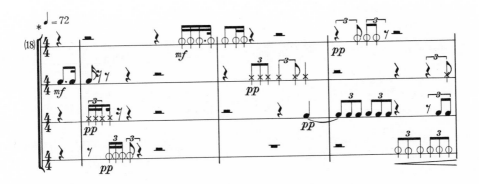

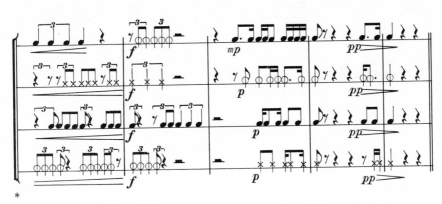

*
⨳ = Clap

φ = Slap

Pitch Sets

Pitch Patterns

Pitch Phrases

✦ = Clap

✟ = Breathy tone

Ukraine

Schumann

212

Allegro appasionato

Grieg

(11)

Mit tiefer Schwermut

Von Kraft

(12)

Allegretto — Rubinstein

(13)

Mit feurigem Schwung — Brahms

(14)

Sweden

(15)

From "La fille aux cheveux de lin."
Durand & Cie, Paris, France copyright owners.
Elkan–Vogel, Inc., agents in the United States

215

Brahms

Debussy

from "Des pas sur la neige."
Durand & Cie, Paris, France copyright owners.
Elkan—Vogel, Inc., agents in the United States

C. P. E. Bach

Fortner

From *Isaak's Opferung*
Copyright © 1952 by B. Schott & Co., Ltd.
Used by permission.

$*$ ↓ $\times$ = Breathy tone

Schubert

From "Prologue." Reprinted by permission of G. Schirmer, Inc.

From "Song of the Harvesters" from *Hiadel*
Copyright 1924 by Universal Edition, Vienna. Renewed 1951.
Copyright assigned to Boosey & Hawkes Ltd. for all countries.
Reprinted by permission of Boosey & Hawkes Inc.

36

J. S. Bach

IMPROVISATION

Invent melodies based on the information provided.

a) G-flat as tonic; b) D-flat as tonic;
c) E-flat as tonic; d) A-flat as tonic.

a) Invent a bass line according to the symbols; then invent a melody in counterpoint to the bass.

b) Play the accompaniment (full texture) and sing the invented melody.

As *2a*, but with the bass line and accompaniment invented by a student other than the performer inventing the melody.

(3)

Use both *P* and *R* forms of the row; begin with either *P* or *R*. Use any of the rhythm phrases appearing in this unit.

Unit 11

RHYTHM: *Introduction of Intrabeat Quadruplets*
PITCH: *Sets Used in Preceding Units*
and Sets Containing Four Consecutive Half Steps
LEAPS: *As in Preceding Units*
TEXTURE: *As in Preceding Units*
RANGE: *Generally an Eleventh*

RHYTHM

Practice Rhythm Patterns

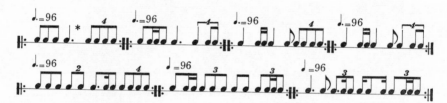

Rhythm Phrases

* Mentally divide ♩. into four equal parts for the quadruplet division.

* Mentally divide the 𝅗𝅥 into three equal parts (𝅘𝅥 𝅘𝅥 𝅘𝅥) in preparation for

the interbeat triplet (𝅗𝅥 𝅗𝅥 𝅗𝅥).

235

237

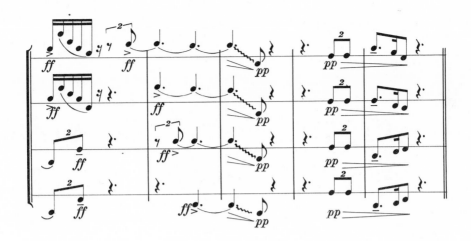

PITCH

Pitch Sets

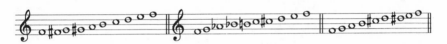

Pitch Patterns

Pitch Phrases

*

$\downarrow$ = Breathy tone

Balfe

242

"Ensourdine." Courtesy of International Music Company, New York, New York.

From *Fifth Nocturne*. © Copyright 1920. Editions Max Eschig. Used by permission of Associated Music Publishers, Inc., agents for the U.S.

Faurè

"Après un rêve." Reprinted by permission of G. Schirmer, Inc.

Debussy

Buxheimer Orgelbuch

From "Spyra," No. 148, Das Buxheimer Orgelbuch in Das Erbe Deutscher Musik. Reprinted by permission of Bärenreiter Verlag.

(22)

(23)

*
⊦ = Tap on book

φ = Slap

✳ = Clap

∧ = Tap

252

Adrian Willaert

us - - que si - ne - bat, ac -

us - que___ si - ne - bat___

- us - que si - ne - bat, ac -

- us - que si - ne - bat, ac -

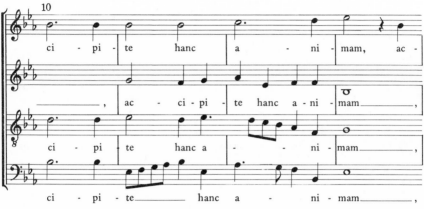

ci - pi - te hanc a - ni - mam, ac -

___, ac - ci - pi - te hanc a - ni - mam___,

ci - pi - te hanc a - ni - mam___,

ci - pi - te___ hanc a - ni - mam___,

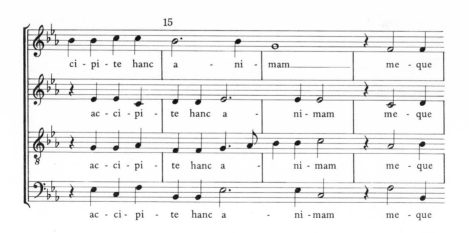

ci - pi - te hanc a - ni - mam___ me - que

ac - ci - pi - te hanc a - ni - mam me - que

ac - ci - pi - te hanc a - ni - mam me - que

ac - ci - pi - te hanc a - ni - mam me - que

his ____ ex - sol - vi - te cu - ris. Vi -

his ex - sol - vi - te ____ cu - ris. Vi -

his ____ ex - sol - vi - te cu - ris. Vi -

his ex - sol - vi - te cu - ris. Vi -

xi et quem de - de - rat cur - sum for - tu - na per -

xi ____ et quem de - de - rat cur - sum for - tu -

xi et quem de - de - rat cur - sum for - tu - na

xi et quem de - de - rat cur - sum for - tu -

e - gi ____ , et nunc mag - na

na ____ per - e - gi, et nunc mag - na

per - e - gi, et nunc

na per - e - gi, et nunc mag - na

IMPROVISATION

Invent melodies with the information given.

a) F as tonic; b) G as tonic; c) B   as tonic

a) Invent a bass line according to the symbols; then invent a melody in counterpoint to the bass.
b) Play the accompaniment (full texture) and sing an invented melody.

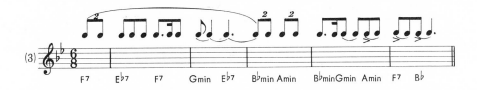

As *2b* but with two performers.

Use both *P* and *I* forms of the row; begin with either *P* or *I*. Use any of the rhythm phrases appearing in this unit.

Unit 12

RHYTHM: *Introduction of Intrabeat Three-Against-Two*
and Four-Against-Three
PITCH: *Sets Used in Preceding Units*
LEAPS: *As in Preceding Units*
TEXTURE: *As in Preceding Units*
RANGE: *Generally a Twelfth*

RHYTHM

Rhythm Phrases

261

264

Pitch Patterns

Pitch Phrases

266

Mexico

(7)

Allegro molto

Bartók

(8)

"Bulgarian Rhythm" from *Mikrokosmos*
Copyright 1941 by Hawkes & Son (London) Ltd. Renewed 1967.
Reprinted by permission of Boosey & Hawkes Inc.

Berlioz

(9)

Un poco allarg.

268

Hindemith

"Wie sankt Franciscus schub' ich in das luft."
Used by permission of B. Schott's Soehne.

Webern

"Bild der Liebe" from *8 Early Songs*. Reprinted by permission of the copyright owner.
Copyright © MCMLXI by Carl Fischer, Inc., New York.
Copyright © MCMLXV by Carl Fischer, Inc., New York.

"L'Ombres des Arbres (Ariettes Oubliees)." Courtesy of International Music Company, New York, New York.

"La fe del ciego." Reprinted by permission of the composer.

From "Sonnet LXXVIII."
Copyright 1942 by Joseph Williams Ltd.
All Rights Reserved.
Used by permission of Galaxy Music Corp., N.Y., sole U.S. agent.

From "Death Came Knocking."
Copyright 1964 by Boosey & Hawkes, Inc.
Reprinted by permission.

ci - pe de - pre - ca - ti - o - nem no - stram.

o - nem no - - - stram.

nem no - - - - stram.

Ockeghem

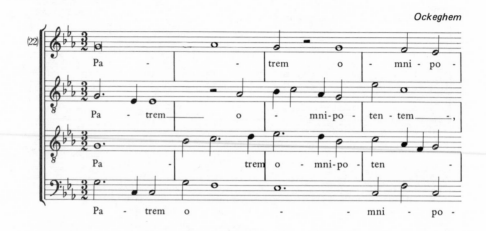

(22) Pa - trem o - mni - po -

Pa - trem o - mni - po - ten - tem,

Pa - trem o - mni - po - ten -

Pa - trem o - - mni - po -

ten - tem, fa - cto-rem coe - li et ter - rae,

fa - cto - rem coe - li,

tem, fa - cto - rem coe - li et ter - rae, vi -

ten - tem, fa - cto - rem coe - li

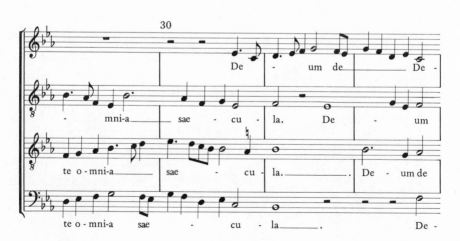

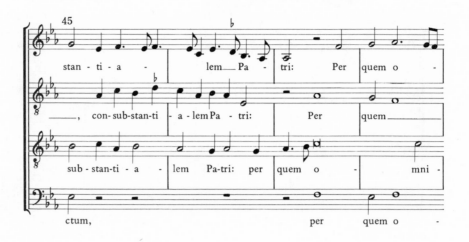

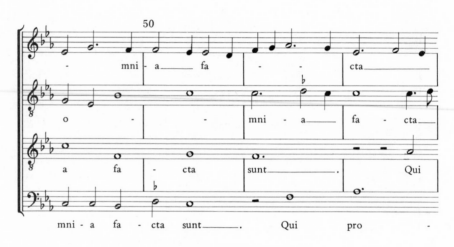

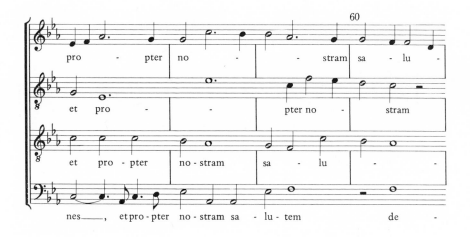

pro - pter no - - stram sa - lu -
et pro - - - pter no - stram
et pro - pter no - stram sa - lu - -
nes___, et pro - pter no - stram sa - lu - tem de -

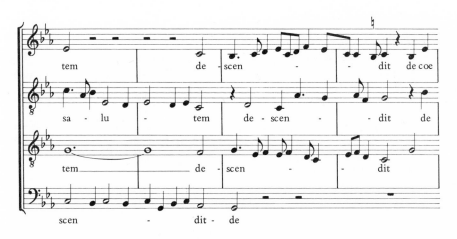

tem de - scen - - dit de coe
sa - lu - tem de - scen - - dit de
tem___ de - scen - - dit
scen - dit - de

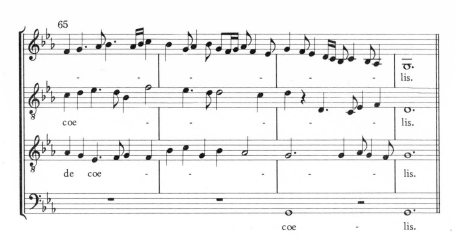

- - - - - lis.
coe - - - - - lis.
de coe - - - - - lis.
coe - lis.

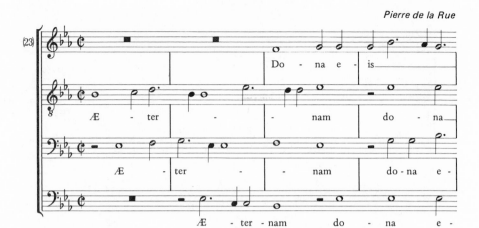

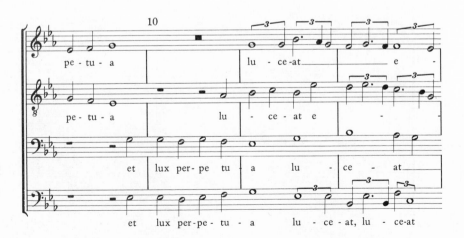

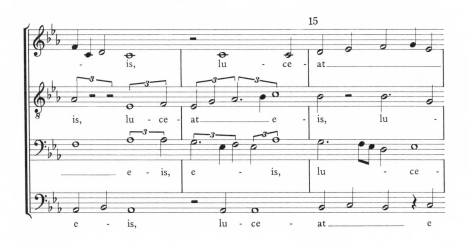

15

Mozart

IMPROVISATION

Invent melodies with the information given.

a) Invent a bass line according to the symbols; then invent a melody in counterpoint to the bass.

b) Play the accompaniment (full texture) and sing an invented melody.

As *2b* but with two performers.

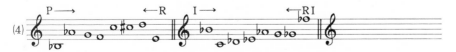

Use *P, R, I,* and *RI* forms of the row; begin with any of the four forms of the row but plan in advance the order in which the row forms are to appear. Use any of the rhythm phrases appearing in this unit (or previous units).

285

Unit 13

RHYTHM: *Continuation of Preceding Units*
PITCH: *Sets Used in Preceding Units*
LEAPS: *As in Preceding Units with Emphasis on Tritone*
TEXTURE: *One to Four Parts*
RANGE: *As in Preceding Unit*

RHYTHM

Practice Rhythm Patterns

Rhythm Phrases

287

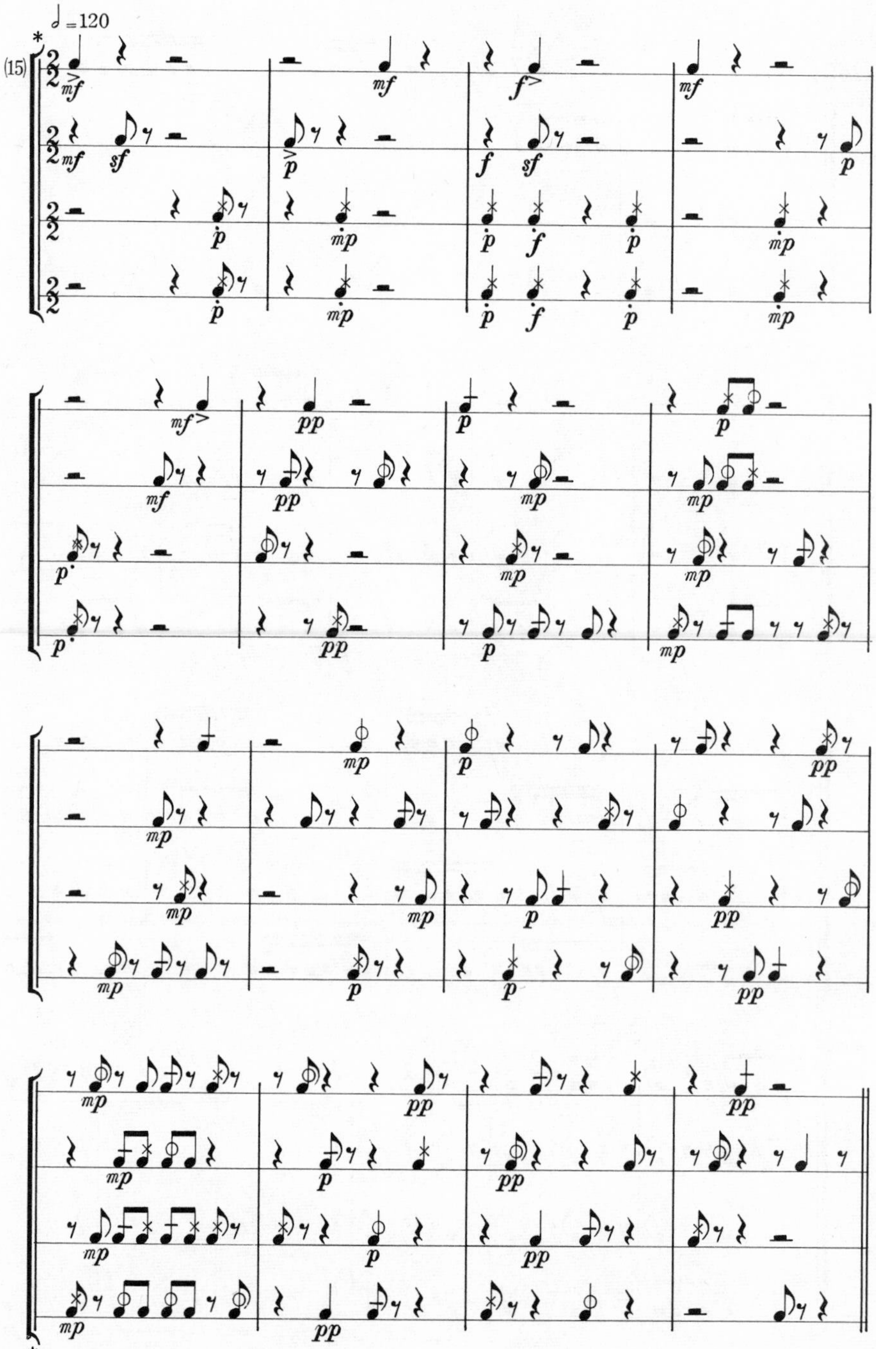

*
♩ = Vocal sounds

𝗑 = Hand clap

⌀ = Slap

┼ = Tap

292

Pitch Phrases

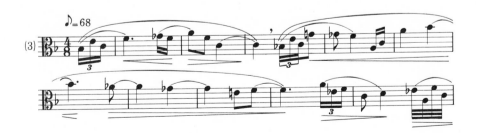

From *Prelude*, Op. 34. Courtesy of International Music Company, New York, New York.

Adagio

Sehr getragen und schwer

H. Wolf

Tempo di marcia

Mahler

From *Revelge*. Copyright, 1905, by C. F. Kahnt

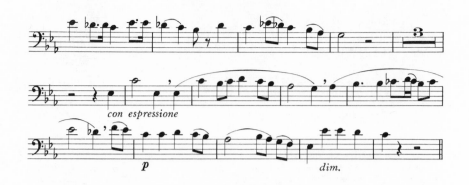

Mässig langsam — Wagner

(14)

Adagio con molto sentimento d'affetto — Beethoven

(15)

mezza voce

espressivo — *cresc.*

dim. — *p*

dimin.

Bewegt und leise — Brahms

(16)

p

Allegro ($\flat.=72$)

Chopin

(17)

mf

scherzando

a tempo

Andante con moto

Fortner

(18)

mp

mf

f

From *Isaak's Opferung*
Copyright © 1952 by B. Schott & Co. Ltd.
Used by permission.

Slowly

Ives

(19) There's a shad - ow on the grass that was nev - er there be - fore;

and the rip - ples as they pass whis - per of an un - seen oar;

And the song we knew by rote, seems to___ fal - ter in the throat,___

a foot - fall, scarce - ly no - ted, lin - gers___ near the o - pen door.

mf
O - mens that were once but jest, Now are mes - sen - gers of Fate;

and the bless - ing held the best___ com - eth not or comes too late.___

mf. faster
Yet what ev - er life may lack, not a blown leaf beck - ons back,

f accel. *ff* *fff*
Forward! For-ward! is the sum - mons. Forward! where new hor - i zons wait.

"Premonitions"
Copyright 1933 by Merion Music, Inc.
Reprinted by permission.

301

J. S. Bach

Herr-scher, Herr, Herr, Herr, un - ser Herr - - -

Herr-scher, Herr, Herr, Herr, un - ser Herr - - -

Herr-scher, Herr, Herr, Herr, un - ser Herr - - -

- scher, Herr, Herr, Herr, un - ser Herr, - - -

Violoncelli e Fagotti

Organo e Violone 6 5   6 4 2   7 4 2   5 4   3   8 4 2   7

25

- - - - - scher, des - sen Ruhm in

- - - - - scher, des - sen Ruhm in

- - - scher, un - ser Herr-scher, des - sen Ruhm in

- - - scher, un - ser Herr - scher, des - sen Ruhm in

8 5   6   8 6 4 2   7 5 2   4   7 5 3 2b   8 ♮

308

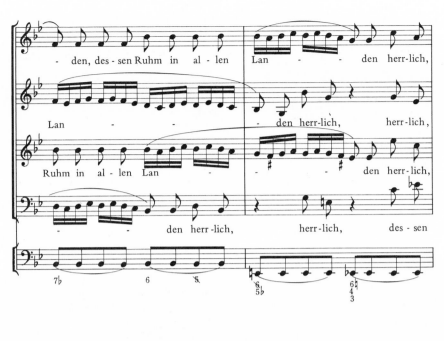

- den, des-sen Ruhm in al - len Lan - - den herr-lich,

Lan - - - den herr-lich, herr-lich,

Ruhm in al - len Lan - - den herr-lich,

- - den herr-lich, herr-lich, des-sen

7♭   6   5   6   6
              5♭   4
                   3

40

herr-lich, herr - lich, herr - lich ist!

herr-lich, herr-lich, herr - lich ist!

herr-lich, herr-lich, herr - lich ist!

Ruhm in al - len Lan - den herr - lich ist!

6   7♭   5
4   5   4
           ♯

IMPROVISATION

Invent melodies with the information given.

* Designates melodic tritones

Sing or play the melody on an instrument; the invented voice uses pitch materials from *1a* and sounds as designated in the fixed patterns.

a) Invent a bass line according to the symbols; then invent a melody in counterpoint to the bass.

b) Play the accompaniment (full texture) and sing the invented melody.

(3)

E F(♭7) E D#min⁷ C#min⁷ F#⁷ B E

A⁷ F#⁷ D#⁷ B⁷ G#⁷ B⁷ E

As *2b* but with two performers.

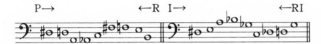

P→ ←R I→ ←RI

Use *P, R, I,* and *RI* forms of the row; begin with any of the four forms of the row but plan the order in which the row forms are to appear. Use any of the rhythm phrases appearing in this unit (or previous units).

Unit 14

RHYTHM: *Introduction of Interbeat Four-Against-Three*
PITCH: *Sets As in Preceding Units*
Sets Containing Five Consecutive Half Steps
LEAPS: *As in Preceding Units*
TEXTURE: *As in Preceding Units*
RANGE: *Generally a Twelfth*

RHYTHM

Rhythm Phrases

* ⨯ = Clap

317

PITCH

Pitch Patterns

Pitch Phrases

(6) Ziemlich langsam   R. Schumann

(7) Adagio   Brahms

(♩.=44)

Giordano

ben cantato

(8) Pas - sa la vi - ta mia   co - me u - na bian - ca   ve - la: essa in -
This life of mine has been   like some en - chan - ted   ves - sel,   and with

cie - la le an - ten - ne   al so - le che le in do - ra   e af -
sails proud-ly fly - ing to greet the gol - den sun - shine, we

fon - da la spu - man - te   pro - ra ne l'az-zur-ro del - l'on-da....
sailed ov - er the dark blue wat - ers of the bil -low-ing o - cean!

Va la mia na - ve spin-ta dal - la sor - te a la sco -
Will my frail barque be dri-ven by mis - for - tune up - on the

glie - ra bian - ca de la mor - te? Son giun-to? Sia!
ghost-ly rocks of death's do - min - ion. and per-ish? May be!

Ma a pop - pa io sal - go e u - na ban - die - ra trion-fa-le sciol-go ai
But there you will see me, proudly un - furl - ing, a - mid the rag-ing

ven - ti, e su vi è scrit-to "Pa - tria!„ A lei non
temp - est, the glo - rious flag of France! No shame-ful

più mosso

sa - le il tuo fan - go! Non sono un tra - di -
ty - rant can de - file it! I swear I am no

deciso

to - re. Uc - ci - di? Ma la - scia-mi l'o - nor!
trait - or! You'd kill - me? Then let me die with hon - our!

From *Andrea Chenier*. Reprinted by permission of Casa Musicale
Sonzogno di Piero Ostali

From *Sonata for Violoncello and Piano,* Op. 12. Used by permission of MCA Music, A division of MCA, Inc.
445 Park Avenue, New York, N.Y. 10022
All Rights Reserved

Très lent   Chausson

"L'Aveu," Op. 13, No. 2. Courtesy of International Music Company, New York, New York.

Assez lent   Saint-Saëns

327

Joyeusement animé

Debussy

(13)

"Aquarelle No. 1"
Copyright MCMXIII by Oliver Ditson Company
Reprinted by Permission

Mässig langsam

Wagner

(14)

From *Die Sache Makropulos.*
Copyright 1926 by Universal Edition
Copyright renewed 1954 by Universal Edition
Reprinted by permission of the publisher. Theodore Presser Company sole representative in the United States, Canada & Mexico.

"Die trundene Tanngerin."
Used by permission of B. Schott's Soehne

Die Achtel etwas lebhafter als vorher die Viertel

sempre cresc.

Wie am Anfang

(♩ = 36)

Dallapiccola

(17)

cresc. molto

From *Frammenti di Saffo, No. III*. Reprinted by permission of Edizioni Suvini Zerboni Milano.

(18)

330

Allegro con brio   Haydn

* ↓ = Breathy tone

↓ = Clap

Andante sostenuto

From *Serenade for Oboe, Viola, and Bassoon*, Op. 36, I. Reprinted by permission of the copyright owner, Dan Fog Musik Forlag, Copenhagen.

336

Grave

Brahms

IMPROVISATION

Invent melodies with the information given.

1. Use any of the two-part rhythmic exercises of this unit as a basis for melodic inventions. The pitch materials should be derived from those given below, or in the unit. a) The upper part invents the melody; the lower part performs as notated in the exercise selected; b) the lower part invents the melody; the upper part is used as rhythmic accompaniment.

2. Invent melodies based on the chord progression given below. Before beginning, decide on the meter, the basic rhythmic patterns to be used, the tempo, and whether there will be one or two performers.

Adapted from Beethoven, Piano Concerto No.4, II

3. Invent melodies based on the progression designated with the symbols given below. Include in the melody various duple patterns.

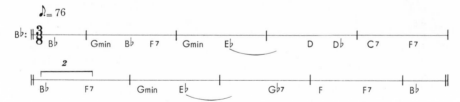

4. Use *P, R, I,* and *RI* forms of the row; begin with any of the four forms of the row (but plan the order in which the row forms are to appear). Use any of the rhythm phrases appearing in this unit (or previous units).

339

Index of Musical Examples